This Journal Be

Printed in Great Britain
by Amazon

35593461R00066